# Love

Lychheng Poch

BookLeaf
Publishing

Presentation by *BookLeaf Publishing*

Web: www.bookleafpub.com

E-mail: info@bookleafpub.com

ISBN: 9789395756235

First edition 2022

# DEDICATION

To my inner child

We are stronger than ever

I love you

# ACKNOWLEDGEMENT

I like to acknowledge the people of the Kulin nation on whose land we are gathered here today. I also like to pay my respect to the elders past, present and emerging.

# Star

Admiring from a far,
It's like looking at a star,
You light up my whole night,
Even when I'm not feeling so bright,
Thinking of you just makes me feel mad,
because I hate being sad,
knowing that I could never have you,
because I'm not you type boo,
you go for them girls,
beautiful, elegant, intelligent,
and damn I wish I was all that,
you're like at the top of the sky,
while look at you with admiring eyes,
I hate acting like a fool,
Whenever I'm near you,
It seems like I lost my speech,
not knowing how to speak,
can't tell you my sense of need,
feeling my heart skips a beat,
To fearful to speak,
to shy to flirt,
how can I say those three little words,
when I can't even say a simple word,
I just wish this year could end,
so I'll never see you again.

# Pain

At night she couldn't sleep
thinking too much and feeling weak
like no one would ever get her
she's living in a house but not a home
she hates feeling all alone
something is obviously missing
hating the sound of her stepdad dissing
she always wondered why
the reason he's never satisfied
with everything she provide
she does everything that she can
at least she tried
from cleaning the house to cutting the grass
but it never seems to be enough
useless, dumb
all the names that's making her numb
telling herself to hold it together
cry when they think you're under the weather
don't ever let him know
how he affected you so
making a crumble
just smile through the pain
telling herself it's you to blame
it wasn't his fault
he was just stating his thoughts

I don't even know why I try
maybe I just hate not knowing why
the reason behind those raging eyes
I just wish I could say goodbye
to this so-called life.

# Beautiful

I hate feeling alone
not being alone, truely alone
at night it all sink in
the feeling inside within
looking into the mirror, feeling terrified
at the reflection inside
is that me? Looking so sad
the girl once had a light in her eyes
looking so dead
she never loved what she saw
her face, size nor her height
she dreams of being beautiful
walking up, looking into the mirror
and seeing beautiful
everyday she feels unsatisfied
at what she's looking at inside
waking up everyday feels like torture
looking into the mirror
not seeing beautiful
why can't she be beautiful?
all she wanted was to feel beautiful.

# Black

My heart feel with darkness
I cannot see
The bitterness, hatred within me
Fury and frustration I cannot show
Something had obviously awoken deep bellow
Maybe it's the monster deep inside of me
Which lead me to believe
My soul has been deceived
Pitch black is all I see
No colour left within me.

# Enough

When I'm around others I tends to forget
but when I'm by myself everything seems to be
floating back
that's what I don't get
sadness consumes me
swallowing me alive
I tried to fight, to escape
but I don't have what it takes
To break
away from this monster
Inside of me
everywhere I go, I hear the voice echos
the voice in my head is getting bold
not smart enough
not pretty enough
not skinny enough
not good enough
just not enough
never enough
why aren't I enough?

# Alone

I hate feeling pathetic,
Crying myself hysteric,
Weak to the bone,
Defeated and feeling so alone,
Crushed of any spirit,
Fucked up beyond repair,
Dysfunctional and feeling despair,
Isolated from pairs,
Scared siting in the dark pulling my hair,
Lost thinking the world so unfair,
Alone because no one cares.

# Blood

He came home one day
angry at something my mum says
those cold and fiery eyes
walking by
grabbing a knife
threatened my life
making me shiver with fears
"Do you want blood on your foods?"
running the knife along my neck
with the sharp object
rooted at the spot
after that plot
he walked away
like it's just another day
I couldn't breath
it came quick and unsteady
like there's no air
no ventilation left there.

# Fantasy

The engine stops
so I drop
my book and rushed to the door
not quick enough he'll be angry for sure
before even the clock tick
voice raising
glass breaking
cowardly I ran
looking the door on the man
more yelling
wall punching
trying to break down my door
sitting in the corner feeling so unsure
I wish everything would be like before
without him
It seems like a dream
a fantasy
far away from what it seems
I wish I could just disappear
God I wish I never have to come back here.

# Hope

Hope, four letter words yet so powerful
outshine others so beautiful
like a light at the end of darkness
a beautiful rainbow when the rain stops
perhaps a beautiful sunshine after every last
drops
clearing the darkness in my soul
bringing back the light
one day my soul will ignites
one day I will not fight
the answer will be shinning bright
in the darkest of the night
survivor is what I'll be
no longer a fragile victim you'll see.

# Monster

So sick of him
Dominating everything
Giving authority on other human beings
Yelling and pointing flaws
Objecting woman like he's the key to open every
door
Making cruel sexist joke
Dismissing it saying he's just being a bloke
Hitting his wife's not showing respect
Instead of protect
Abusing her for little mistakes she makes
He doesn't have what it takes
To be a man
A man would never put a hand
On innocent women
Specially their wife
She supposed to be the love of his life
He's just a sicko
With a fucked up ego
I wish he could die
Burn in hell with a knife in his eyes.

# Trust

I don't trust people in my life
No matter how nice
Doubts always on my mind
Telling myself not to be blind
They always want something
Acting friendly pretending
I don't believe
I hate being deceive
I see through their lies
If I confront them they would deny
Everyone has a motive
Maybe not all are erosive
People doesn't care
About your despair
They don't want their time wasted on you
But everyone always need help out of the blue
When it's your turn
They withdrew
It's like déjà vu
I should have guessed
I shouldn't protest or be depressed
Acceptance it is the key
to be free
Just don't believe them when they're nice
Because they'll just ask for your help thrice.

# Happy

Done fighting
Tired of trying
Go your own way
I won't ask you to stay
It's my fault
my automatic default
Self destruct is my speciality
All I do is stay unhappy
Unloved is all I'll be
Because I can't seem to love me
I'm sorry
I can't trust easily
I'm sorry
It's not you it's me
Seems like god is playing a cruel joke on my life
It hurts like a twisting knife
Right person wrong time
How many more obstacle to I have to climb ?
Is it a crime to want happiness?
It's getting hard being an optimist
It's Getting harder to feel
It's even harder to love if you can't heal

# Anger

Anger, hatred towards the sky
The sun mocking me with tears pulling in my
eyes
Why do you hate me so?
You left me shivering in the snow
Alone in the darkness of the night
I tried to fight, to escape
But I never have what it takes
You said I was your daughter
Yet you never even bother
To check on my soul
It's turning dark, can't you see?
Breathing normally but not free
Conflicts within me
Drowning, suffocating
I guess maybe it's just me
I forgot how to truly be free
Doubts always on my mind
Do I take your hand or let you go?
I just don't know.

# Strong

One thing I've learned
If you don't want to get burned
Rely on what you earned
No amounts of tears
Will make the reality unreal
So sit down, relax and grab a beer
There's no such thing as fairytales
Don't you stay in bed and wail
No one is going to save you, let alone a male
Prince Charming? He probably in bed with
another female
Knight in shining armour? Probably somewhere
being blackmailed or in jail
The reality of escaping hell
Rely within yourself
Don't dwell or yell
That life isn't fair
Don't you dare
You do not need nobody I swear
You alone is strong enough to get out of that
nightmare.

# Ly

I have these thoughts in my head
I dread to let it fled
People might say it's mad
Someday I want to marry a lad
Like Glenn
But I also want to marry me a girl like Gwen
There I said it again
The first time I thought about a girl was year 10
I didn't know what It meant
I was petrified at the turn of event
I shut it down then
My justification was I still like men
I refuse to think about girls again until high
school nearly end
I still didn't know what it meant
I didn't understand
Why can't I focus on liking a man?
I was more informed yet still feel afraid and less
than
I started to question my own sincerity
Maybe I was doing it for attention
Maybe I'm doing it to give my life some
dimension
I gave myself a much needed convention

How will you get attention if u haven't told
your closest peers
It was the fear
I can see it now crystal clear
I needed to accept myself for who i am
Before telling others who I am
Now I know who I am
I told my two closest friends
It wasn't a phase nor trend
This part of me is not my whole identity
I try to explain this sensibly
But it is a part of my identity
I emphasise this breathlessly
Thankfully, to them I was still just Ly.

# Love

See what happened was
I saw something in you that made me paused
I got scared and I withdraws
There was something about your looks that
scream outlaws
I don't understand why I was in awe
I don't know what I saw
That drew me into the devils claws
I tried to get out some more
I tried my best to ignore
I walked and went next door
But he wasn't someone I was looking for
He wasn't you I'm sure
I came back feeling like a whore
I broke him but I wanted you more
It was selfish but I couldn't lie to myself
anymore
Being with you never felt like a chore
I was high on you and I wanted some more
A beautiful broken man is what I saw
Your pain, guilt and shame I wanted it all
I started to fall
But you builded a wall
It wasn't a surprising curve ball

I guess that was my downfall
I hope you find what you're looking for
I have to stop playing pretend
That we were more than what's intend
In the end,
I was just an easy lady friend
It was hard to comprehend
But I finally see it crystal clear
Maybe that's my lesson for this year
Please take care of yourself
Sincerely
One of your peers

# Kicks

Our first encounter was at kicks
We talked and seemed to clicked
I felt something then but I knew it was too quick
Found out you had a girl I felt conflict
We both went our separate way but stayed in the
same cliques
You broke up with her and got with a new chick
I would be lying if I said I didn't feel that kicked
Promised myself to move on and founded a new
dick
I thought he was just a temporary pick
I started to fall, guess I wasn't too slick
So much tequila till I was so sick
You had issues with her and thought I was a
quick fix
I had issues with him and thought you were a
quick fix
Told you we ain't it
I tried but knew we were a misfit
Hypocrite
You threw a fit
But you told me the same shit
U knew your friends won't like me admit
You say you'll cut them off in a bit
I don't want that shit

You don't understand me even a little bit
I knew it was only right to split
I thought you would just go off the grid
But u decided to slit
Your wrist and say u quit
Your life and asked me to watch it
Said I made my bed now I gotta lie in it
Deal with it
u made me this way bitch
I couldn't bear it
All I wanted was to quit
But you got through it
You then later told me I wasn't it
You were hurt from your ex
So you took it out on the next
Guess u didn't like getting reject
Hey thanks for that
My first dick wasn't perfect
I Gotta admit
Not a bad story to tell my grandkids

# Me

Dear: Me
Who knew we would be here today
All the countless night left in dismay
Drinking and got faded everyday
Just to feel something, Saturdays
Trying to find a little happiness with Vitamins A
Black out on Valentines Day
Kissing strangers like it's just another day
Got caught up in a drama, action replay
But what you couldn't understand
Something you never demand
The respect you deserve beforehand
You walked in this world hating yourself
Actively killing oneself
Soulless slowly killing herself
No more, put those thoughts on the shelf
Lock it up and throw away the keys
Someday I still feel unease
Eating me up like a disease
But someday I feel at ease
I'm still learning to love me
I'm learning to truely be free
I'm learning to love what I see
Like a kid, I'm starting with my abc...

# Sorry

I thought I was ready
to be loved in my twenties
you were sweet and it was all dandy
we drove around holding hands all happy
you were picture perfect all manly
you took me out, show me off all proudly
I'm not it for you sadly
I want to feel alive, giddy, messy
exploding passion, heavy, deadly
I want to fall in love unexpectedly
not forced nor calculated, barely
a love that drives me unsteady
nothing about it would be ordinary
I thought it could be you momentarily
but I couldn't feel my heart beating unwary
being with you was friendly
I still feel alone, envy
I had to let you go gently
I'm sorry, please don't hate me
I want to experience life to an adequate degree
I want to sightsee and be set free
I want to follow my heart finally
I want to choose me

# Win

I'm healing
I took time to sit with my feeling
Instead of concealing
I'm so glad I was dealing
Because when I met you it was revealing
I'm in the process of self healing
You treat me right I keep receiving
You help me close without deceiving
You made me feel secure achieving
You never left me grieving
Always telling me when you're leaving
I'm starting to believe in
That sweet grin
I can feel it within
A win.

# Together

You looked great on the dance floor
You pulled my hair and my body roared
I had to ignore
I've never looked at you that way before
I couldn't stay away anymore
You helped me out the door
We went to yours
You slept on the floor
Rejecting my request to explore
Refused to treat me like a whore
I hate my nose but you seem to adore
You made me laugh till I swore
You have a kind side furthermore
I hope this doesn't turn into a war.